PEACE

Quotations & Aspirations

PEACE
Quotations & Aspirations

Compiled & Edited by
Tammy Ruggles

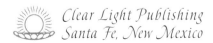

Clear Light Publishing
Santa Fe, New Mexico

This book is dedicated to my granddaughter, Destiny.

Copyright 2006 by Tammy Ruggles
Clear Light Publishing
823 Don Diego
Santa Fe, New Mexico 87505
www.clearlightbooks.com

First Edition
10 9 8 7 6 5 4 3 2 1

Library of Congress Cataloging-in-Publication Data

Peace : quotes & aspirations for a peaceful planet / compiled & edited by Tammy Ruggles.
    p. cm.
  Includes bibliographical references and index.
  ISBN 1-57416-083-4
  1. Peace—Quotations, maxims, etc. I. Ruggles, Tammy.
  pn6084.p45p45 2004
  327.1'72--dc22

                                                    2004022036

Dove, display lettering & cover design by Judythe Sieck
Interior design by Marcia Keegan & Carol O'Shea

TABLE OF CONTENTS

VISIONS OF PEACE

Imagine all the people living life in peace...

JOHN LENNON
British singer/songwriter

*A day will come when a cannon will be exhibited in museums,
just as instruments of torture are now, and the people will be
astonished that such a thing could have been.*

VICTOR HUGO
French writer

Peace comes within the souls of men when they realize their oneness with the universe.

BLACK ELK
Oglala Sioux spiritual leader

Embrace perfect peace. The world will rise and move; watch it return to rest.

TAO TE CHING
Taoist scripture

Mankind must remember that peace is not God's gift to his creatures, peace is our gift to each other.

ELIE WIESEL
Romanian journalist and winner of the Nobel Peace Prize

When the power of love overcomes the love of power
the world will know peace.

JIMI HENDRIX

(1942–1970) American musician, guitarist, singer and songwriter

All the arms we need are for hugging.

AUTHOR UNKNOWN

Therefore, the various souls relate to one another as parts of one
body; and from this point of view, the higher a person rises, the
trials and difficulties involved are increasingly concerned with
one's fellow man. For every human being is a part of the single soul
that is the spirit of the entire universe.

ADIN STEINSALTZ

Hebrew author and founder of the Israel Institute for Talmudic Publications

At the center of non-violence stands the principle of love.

MARTIN LUTHER KING, JR.
American clergyman, civil rights leader and Nobel Peace Prize winner

This we know, the earth does not belong to us.
We belong to the earth.
This we know, all things are connected. Like the blood which
unites one family, all things are connected.
Our God is the same God, whose compassion is equal for all.
For we did not weave the web of life.
We are merely a strand in it.
Whatever we do to the web, we do to ourselves.
Let us give thanks for the web and the circle that connects us.
Thanks be to God, the God of all.

CHIEF SEATTLE
Suquamish and Duwamish Indian chief and spiritual leader

... the "Sigh of Compassion" flows through the things of the world like the waters of a river and is unceasingly renewed.

IBN AL-ARABI
Sufi mystic

In India when we meet and part we often say, "Namaste," which means I honor the place in you where the entire universe resides; I honor the place in you of love, of light, of truth, of peace. I honor the place within you where if you are in that place in you and I am in that place in me, there is only one of us... "Namaste."

RAM DASS
American author and spiritual teacher

My humanity is bound up in yours, for we can only be human together.

ARCHBISHOP DESMOND TUTU
South African clergyman, civil rights activist and winner of the Nobel Peace Prize

In Beauty, may I walk. All day long, may I walk.
Through the returning seasons, may I walk.
On the trail marked with pollen, may I walk.
With grasshoppers about my feet, may I walk.
With dew about my feet, may I walk.
With beauty, may I walk.
With Beauty before me, may I walk.
With Beauty behind me, may I walk.
With Beauty above me, may I walk.
With Beauty below me, may I walk.
With Beauty all around me, may I walk.
In old age wandering on a trail of beauty, lively, may I walk.
In old age wandering on a trail of beauty, living again,
may I walk.
It is finished in Beauty.
It is finished in Beauty.

BEAUTY WAY PRAYER FROM THE NAVAJO TRADITION

Imagine a hoop so large that everything is in it—all two-leggeds like us, four-leggeds, the fishes of the streams, the wings of the air, and all green things that grow. Everything is together in this great hoop.

BLACK ELK

Oglala Sioux spiritual leader

Until he extends his circle of compassion to include all living things, man will not himself find peace.

ALBERT SCHWEITZER

French medical missionary, theologian, musician and philosopher

The ultimate spiritual issue of our age is saving God's creation.

HELEN CALDICOTT

Australian physician and peace activist

I believe that man will not merely endure: he will prevail. He is immortal, not because he alone among creatures has an inexhaustible voice, but because he has a soul, a spirit capable of compassion and sacrifice and endurance. The poet's, the writer's, duty is to write about these things. It is his privilege to help man endure by lifting his heart, by reminding him of the courage and honor and hope and pride and compassion and pity and sacrifice which have been the glory of his past. The poet's voice need not merely be the record of man, it can be one of the props, the pillars to help him endure and prevail.

WILLIAM FAULKNER
American author and winner of Nobel Prize for Literature

We shall find peace. We shall hear angels, we shall see the sky sparkling with diamonds.

ANTON CHEKHOV
Russian playwright

Some men see things as they are and say why...I dream of things that never were and say why not.

GEORGE BERNARD SHAW

Irish playwright and essayist

Great ideas, it has been said, come into the world as gently as doves. Perhaps then, if we listen attentively, we shall hear amid the uproar of empires and nations, a faint flutter of wings, a gentle stirring of life and hope. Some will say that this hope lies in a nation; others in a person. I believe rather that it is awakened, revived, nourished by millions of solitary individuals whose deeds and works every day negate frontiers and the crudest implications of history. As a result, there shines forth fleetingly the ever-threatened truth that each and every person, on the foundation of his or her own sufferings and joys, builds for all.

ALBERT CAMUS

French philosopher, novelist and playwright

No more wars, no more bloodshed. Peace unto you.
Shalom, salaam, forever.

MENACHEM BEGIN
Former prime minister of Israel and winner of the Nobel Peace Prize

As we grow in awareness of one another—whether two people beginning a romance or two disparate and far-removed strangers taking an interest in the other's culture—a wonderful thing begins to happen: we begin to care for the other as if the other is part of us. This is the magic of life that our ancient teachers have bid us to see; the invisible filaments of interconnectedness that bind us together in love and appreciation.

SCOTT A. HUNT
American writer and philosopher

No despair of ours can alter the reality of things, or stain the joy of the cosmic dance which is always there.

THOMAS MERTON
Catholic monk and spiritual writer

The first and highest law must be the love of man to man.
Homo homini Deus est — this is the supreme practical maxim, this
is the turning point of the world's History.

LUDWIG FEUERBACH
German philosopher

Peace is not the absence of war; it is a virtue; a state of mind;
a disposition for benevolence; confidence; and justice.

SPINOZA
Philosopher and theologian from the Netherlands

[Peace] is more than the absence of war. Peace, in fact, is
not the absence of anything, but rather the
ultimate affirmation of what can be.

RABBI KENNETH L. COHEN
American writer and peace activist

*A great vision is needed and the man who has it must follow it
as the eagle seeks the deepest blue of the sky.*

CRAZY HORSE
Oglala Sioux chief

*Peace is an active presence of the capacity for a
higher evolution of human awareness.*

DENNIS KUCINICH
U.S. representative from Ohio and peace activist

*Peace will come wherever it is sincerely invited. Love will overflow
every sanctuary given it. Truth will grow where the fertilizer that
nourishes it is also truth. Faith will be its own reward.*

ALICE WALKER
American novelist and poet

Let us plant dates even though those who plant them will never eat them. We must live by the love of what we will never see. This is the secret discipline. It is a refusal to let the creative act be dissolved away in immediate sense experience, and a stubborn commitment to the future of our grandchildren. Such disciplined love is what has given prophets, revolutionaries, and saints the courage to die for the future they envisaged. They make their own bodies the seed of their highest hope.

RUBEM ALVES
Brazilian author, philosopher and writer of children's books

May we be nourished together. May we work together. May our studies be brilliant. May we not fight with each other.
Peace. Peace. Peace.

"SHANTI MANTRA" PRAYERS
Vedic peace prayers

May all beings everywhere
with whom we are inseparably connected,
be fulfilled, awakened, liberated and free.
May there be peace in this world
and throughout the entire universe,
and may we all together
complete the spiritual journey.

PRAYER FROM THE MAHAYANA BUDDHIST TRADITION

O Lord, my God,
grant us your peace; already, indeed,
you have made us rich in all things!
Give us that peace of being at rest,
that sabbath peace,
the peace which knows no end.

ST. AUGUSTINE

North African bishop & saint and a founding father of Western thought

I desire neither earthly kingdom,
nor even freedom from birth and death.
I desire only the deliverance
from grief of all those afflicted by misery.
Oh Lord, lead us from the unreal to the real;
from darkness to light,
from death to immortality.
May there be peace in celestial regions.
May there be peace on earth.
May the waters be appeasing.
May herbs be wholesome
And may trees and plants bring peace to all.
May all beneficent beings bring peace to us.
May thy wisdom spread peace all through the world.
May all things be a source of peace to all and to me.

PEACE PRAYER FROM THE HINDU TRADITION

Dear God, Please send to me the spirit of Your peace. Then send, dear Lord, the spirit of peace from me to all the world. Amen.

MARIANNE WILLIAMSON
American author and peace advocate

Pray not for Arab or Jew,
For Palestinian or Israeli,
But pray rather for yourselves
That you may not divide them in your prayers,
But keep them both together in your hearts.

RABBI STANLEY A. RINGLER
Israeli writer and peace advocate

And the servants of the God of Mercy are they who walk upon the Earth softly, and when the ignorant address them, they reply, Peace!

QURAN (KORAN)
The holy book of Islam

May faith and love of God make the followers of every religion courageous builders of understanding and forgiveness, patient weavers of a fruitful inter-religious dialogue, capable of inaugurating a new era of justice and peace.

POPE JOHN PAUL II

May my house be in harmony
From my head, may it be happy
To my feet, may it be happy
Where I lie, may it be happy
All above me, may it be happy
All around me, may it be happy.

PEACE PRAYER FROM THE NAVAJO TRADITION

There will be peace on earth when there is peace among the world religions.

HANS KÜNG
Swiss Roman Catholic priest and theologian

The Art of Peace functions everywhere on earth, in realms ranging from the vastness of space down to the tiniest plants and animals. The life force is all-pervasive and its strength boundless. The Art of Peace allows us to perceive and tap into that tremendous reserve of universal energy.

MORIHEI UESHIBA
Japanese martial arts expert and founder of Aikido

Whether we can evolve emotionally and psychologically and spiritually in time to save ourselves and all other species on the planet — I don't know, but I believe we can.

HELEN CALDICOTT
Australian physician and peace activist

It'll be a great day when education gets all the money it wants and the Air Force has to hold a bake sale to buy bombers.

AUTHOR UNKNOWN

Take heaven! No peace lies in the future which is not hidden in this present little instant. Take peace! The gloom of the world is but a shadow. Behind it, yet within our reach, is joy.

GIOVANNI GIOCONDO
Italian architect, writer, archaeologist and classical scholar

Sometime they'll give a war and nobody will come.

CARL SANDBURG
American poet

INNER PEACE

Without inner peace, it is impossible to have world peace.

THE DALAI LAMA
Tibetan Buddhist spiritual and temporal leader and winner of the Nobel Peace Prize

Create each day anew by clothing yourself with heaven and earth, bathing yourself with wisdom and love, and placing yourself in the heart of Mother Nature.

MORIHEI UESHIBA
Japanese martial arts expert and founder of Aikido

The only way to end all wars is the inner peace of each one of us.

RUBEN FELDMAN GONZALEZ
Argentine physician and lecturer

If there is to be peace in the world,
There must be peace in the nations.
If there is to be peace in the nations,
There must be peace in the cities.
If there is to be peace in the cities,
There must be peace between neighbors.
If there is to be peace between neighbors,
There must be peace in the home.
If there is to be peace in the home,
There must be peace in the heart.

LAO-TSE
Chinese Philosopher, 6th Century BC

Everything that has a beginning has an ending.
Make your peace with that and all will be well.

THE BUDDHA

O God, make us children of quietness,
and heirs of peace.

ST. CLEMENT OF ROME

Pope, first ecclesiastical writer to be called Apostolic Father

Better indeed is knowledge than mechanical practice (of religious ritual). Better than knowledge is meditation. But better still is surrender of attachment to results (of one's actions), because there follows immediate peace.

THE BHAGAVAD-GITA

Sacred scripture of ancient India

*What is Faith? When your good deed pleases you and your evil
deed grieves you, you are a believer. What is Sin? When a thing
disturbs (the peace of) your heart, give it up.*

MUHAMMAD

Muslim prophet and founder of Islam

*A mind at peace, a mind focused on not harming others,
is stronger than any physical force in the universe.*

DR. WAYNE DYER

American author/motivational speaker

*Although it is difficult to bring about peace through internal
transformation, this is the only way to achieve lasting world
peace. Even if during my lifetime it is not achieved, it is all right.
The next generation will make more progress.*

THE DALAI LAMA

Tibetan Buddhist spiritual and temporal leader and winner of the Nobel Peace Prize

When someone at peace and free from hurry enters a room,
that person has a calming effect on everyone present.

EKNATH EASWARAN

Meditation teacher and founder of Blue Mountain Center of Meditation

If we are peaceful,
If we are happy,
we can blossom like a flower,
and everyone in our family,
In our entire society,
will benefit from our peace.

THICH NHAT HANH

Vietnamese Buddhist monk and peace activist

He who knows patience knows peace.

CHINESE PROVERB

The life of inner peace, being harmonious and without stress,
is the easiest type of existence.

NORMAN VINCENT PEALE

American religious leader

Peace is not a relationship of nations. It is a condition of mind
brought about by a serenity of soul. Peace is not merely
the absence of war. It is also a state of mind.
Lasting peace can come only to peaceful people.

JAWAHARLAL NEHRU

Indian statesman and prime minister

First keep thyself in peace, and then shalt thou be able
to be a peacemaker towards others.

THOMAS À KEMPIS

German monk and theologian

It is essential to know that to be a happy person, a happy family, a happy society, it is very crucial to have a good heart, that is very crucial. World peace must develop from inner peace. Peace is not just the absence of violence but the manifestation of human compassion.

THE DALAI LAMA
Tibetan Buddhist spiritual and temporal leader and winner of the Nobel Peace Prize

*While you are proclaiming peace with your lips,
be careful to have it even more fully in your heart.*

ST. FRANCIS OF ASSISI
Patron saint of animals and the environment, founder of the Franciscan Order

Nothing can bring you peace but yourself.

RALPH WALDO EMERSON
merican author, minister and activist

*Go placidly amid the noise and the haste,
and remember what peace there may be in silence.*

MAX EHRMANN
American poet and essayist

In the hearts of people today there is a deep longing for peace. When the true spirit of peace is thoroughly dominant, it becomes an inner experience with unlimited possibilities. Only when this really happens—when the spirit of peace awakens and takes possession of men's hearts, can humanity be saved from perishing.

ALBERT SCHWEITZER
French medical missionary, theologian, musician and philosopher

The real change must happen within us. For only when conflict and negativity are removed from within can we play a truly constructive role in establishing peace.

AMMACHI
Indian yogic spiritual teacher

Peace originates with the flow of things—its heart is like the movement of the wind and waves. The Way is like the veins that circulate blood through our bodies, following the natural flow of the life force. If you are separated in the slightest from that divine essence, you are far off the path.

MORIHEI UESHIBA
Japanese martial arts expert and founder of Aikido

The first peace, which is the most important, is that which comes within the souls of people when they realize their relationship, their oneness with the universe and all its powers, and when they realize that at the center of the universe dwells the Great Spirit, and that this center is really everywhere, it is within each of us.

BLACK ELK
Oglala Sioux spiritual leader

Man must feel the earth to know himself and recognize his values...God made life simple. It is man who complicates it.

CHARLES A. LINDBERGH
American pilot, inventor, author and environmentalist

Remember, don't waste time comparing your life to others who seem more fortunate. Being fortunate is based on how much peace you have, not how many luxuries or conveniences you have. Practice from the heart to make peace with what is, then life gives you more help to change things for the better.

DOC CHILDRE
American author of self-help and self-discovery books

Other people do not have to change for us to experience peace of mind.

GERALD JAMPOLSKY, M.D.
Author & founder of Center for Attitudinal Healing

When we are capable of living in the moment free from the tyranny of "shoulds," free from the nagging sensation that this moment isn't right, we will have peaceful hearts.

JOAN BORYSENKO
American author of spiritual self-help books

If you haven't forgiven yourself something, how can you forgive others?

DOLORES HUERTA
Mexican-American co-founder of United Farm Workers with César Chávez

Never be in a hurry; do everything quietly and in a calm spirit. Do not lose your inner peace for anything whatsoever, even if your whole world seems upset.

ST. FRANCIS DE SALES
Roman Catholic bishop and writer

Reshape yourself through the power of your will...
Those who have conquered themselves...
live in peace, alike in cold and heat,
pleasure and pain, praise and blame...
To such people a clod of dirt, a stone, and gold are the same...
Because they are impartial, they rise to great heights.

THE BHAGAVAD GITA
Sacred scripture of ancient India

And once we have the condition of peace and joy in us, we can afford to be in any situation. Even in the situation of hell, we will be able to contribute our peace and serenity. The most important thing is for each of us to have some freedom in our heart, some stability in our heart, some peace in our heart. Only then will we be able to relieve the suffering around us.

THICH NHAT HANH
Vietnamese Buddhist monk and peace activist

Peace does not mean to be in a place where there is no noise, trouble or hard work. Peace means to be in the midst of all those things and still be calm in your heart. That is the real meaning of peace.

AUTHOR UNKNOWN

People spend a lifetime searching for happiness; looking for peace. They chase idle dreams, addictions, religions, even other people, hoping to fill the emptiness that plagues them. The irony is the only place they ever needed to search was within.

RAMONA L. ANDERSON

You are seeking joy and peace in far-off places. But the spring of joy is in your heart. The haven of peace is in yourself.

SATYA SAI BABA
Hindu spiritual teacher

Peace comes from within. Do not seek it without.

THE BUDDHA

Indecision regarding the choice among pleasures temporarily robs a man of inner peace. After due reflection, he attains joy by turning away from the lower pleasures and seeking the higher ones.

I CHING

Ancient Chinese book of Confucianism

As I have said, the first thing is to be honest with yourself. You can never have an impact on society if you have not changed yourself... Great peacemakers are all people of integrity, of honesty, but humility.

NELSON MANDELA

Civil rights activist, former president of South Africa and winner of the Nobel Peace Prize

You can never get to peace and inner security without first acknowledging all of the good things in your life. If you're forever wanting and longing for more without first appreciating things the way they are, you'll stay in discord.

DOC CHILDRE AND HOWARD MARTIN
American authors of self-help and self-discovery books, and

Cultivate peace first in the garden of your heart by removing the weeds of lust, hatred, greed, selfishness, and jealousy. Then only you can manifest it externally. Then only, those who come in contact with you will be benefited by your vibrations of peace and harmony.

SIVANANDA
Indian swami and spiritual teacher

Peace be with you.

JESUS CHRIST
Holy Bible

Whatever you do, you need courage. Whatever course you decide upon, there is always someone to tell you that you are wrong. There are always difficulties arising that tempt you to believe your critics are right. To map out a course of action and follow it to an end requires some of the same courage that a soldier needs. Peace has its victories, but it takes brave men and women to win them.

RALPH WALDO EMERSON
American author, minister and activist

The Art of Peace is medicine for a sick world. There is evil and disorder in the world because people have forgotten that all things emanate from one source. Return to that source and leave behind all self-centered thoughts, petty desires, and anger. Those who are possessed by nothing possess everything.

MORIHEI UESHIBA
Japanese martial arts expert and founder of Aikido

Forgiveness is an inner correction that lightens the heart. It is for our peace of mind first. Being at peace, we will now have peace to give to others, and this is the most permanent and valuable gift we can possibly give.

GERALD JAMPOLSKY, M.D.
Author & founder of Center for Attitudinal Healing

Peace is its own reward.

MAHATMA GANDHI
(Mohandas K. Gandhi) Indian leader and peace activist

May your days be many and your troubles be few.
May all God's blessings descend upon you.
May peace be within you; may your heart be strong.
May you find what you're seeking wherever you roam.

IRISH BLESSING

PROACTIVE PEACE

There is no way to peace. Peace is the way.

A.J. MUSTE

Protestant clergyman from the Netherlands

*Teach this triple truth to all: A generous heart,
kind speech, and a life of service and compassion
are the things which renew humanity.*

THE BUDDHA

Millions of people are ready to join in harmonious interaction with Nature—and with our own complex inner nature—to create a world of peace, harmony, laughter and love. Let us strengthen our intention to create that critical mass of peace consciousness. Every tear can be a drop of nourishment for the new world that wants to be born and is making itself known little by little, every day. Each one of us can help create this critical mass by becoming the embodiment of peace conciousness their peace practices:

Being Peace
Thinking Peace
Feeling Peace
Speaking Peace
Acting Peace
Creating Peace
Sharing Peace
Celebrating Peace.

The Alliance for the New Humanity is committed to connecting and strengthening the synaptic network of the emerging planetary mind.

DEEPAK CHOPRA
American alternative medicine physician and best-selling author

The question of real, lasting world peace concerns human beings, so basic human feelings are also at its roots. Through inner peace, genuine world peace can be achieved. In this the importance of individual responsibility is quite clear; atmosphere of peace must first be created within ourselves, then gradually expanded to include our families, our communities, and ultimately the whole planet.

THE DALAI LAMA
Tibetan Buddhist spiritual and temporal leader and winner of the Nobel Peace Prize

Smiling is very important. If we are not able to smile, then the world will not have peace. It is not by going out for a demonstration against nuclear missiles that we can bring about peace. It is with our capacity of smiling, breathing, and being peace that we can make peace.

THICH NHAT HANH
Vietnamese Buddhist monk and peace activist

*Peace begins with a smile—smile five times a day to someone
you don't really want to smile at all—do it for peace.
So let us radiate the peace of God and so light his light.*

MOTHER TERESA
Albanian Christian missionary in India and winner of the Nobel Peace Prize

*Have you had a kindness shown?
Pass it on;
'Twas not given for thee alone,
Pass it on;
Let it travel down the years,
Let it wipe another's tears,
'Til in Heaven the deed appears
Pass it on.*

HENRY BURTON
English clergyman and writer

Blessed are the peacemakers,
for they shall be known as
the Children of God.
But I say to you that hear,
love your enemies,
do good to those who hate you,
bless those who curse you
pray for those who abuse you.
To those that strike you on the cheek,
offer the other one also
and from those who take away your cloak,
do not withhold your coat as well.
Give to everyone who begs from you,
and of those who take away your goods,
do not ask for them again.
And as you wish that others would do to you,
do so to them.

PEACE PRAYER FROM THE CHRISTIAN TRADITION

Only when there are many people who are pools of peace,
silence and understanding, will war disappear.

OSHO

Indian spiritual leader, a.k.a. Bhagwan Shree Rajneesh

The most faithful disciples of Christ have been builders of peace,
to the point of forgiving their enemies, sometimes even
to the point of giving their lives for them.

POPE JOHN PAUL II

If you wish to be brothers, let the arms fall from your hands.
One cannot love while holding offensive arms.

POPE PIUS VI

Compassion and love are not mere luxuries. As the source of both inner and external peace, they are fundamental to the continued survival of our species.

THE DALAI LAMA
Tibetan Buddhist spiritual and temporal leader and winner of the Nobel Peace Prize

Shall I tell you what acts are better than fasting, charity and prayers? Making peace between enemies are such acts; For enmity and malice tear up the heavenly rewards by the roots.

PRAYER FROM THE ISLAMIC TRADITION

Forgiving those who hurt us is the key to personal peace.

G. WEATHERLY
American writer

*Peace will come only when you yourself are peaceful,
when you yourself are at peace with your neighbour.*

JIDDU KRISHNAMURTI
Indian theosophist

*Be fearless and pure; never waver in your determination or your
dedication to the spiritual life. Give freely. Be self-controlled,
sincere, truthful, loving and full of the desire to serve... Learn to be
detached and to take joy in renunciation. Do not get angry or harm
any living creature, but be compassionate and gentle; show good
will to all. Cultivate vigor, patience, will, purity; avoid malice and
pride. Then, you will achieve your destiny.*

THE BHAGAVAD GITA
Sacred scripture of ancient India

So instead of loving what you think is peace, love other [people] and love God above all. And instead of hating the people you think are warmakers, hate the appetites and the disorder in your own soul, which are the causes of war. If you love peace, then hate injustice, hate tyranny, hate greed—but hate these things in yourself, not in another.

THOMAS MERTON
Catholic monk and spiritual writer

Would that I could be the peacemaker in your soul, that I might turn the discord and the rivalry of your elements into oneness and melody. But how shall I, unless you yourselves be also the peacemakers, nay, the lovers of all your elements?

KAHIL GIBRAN
Syrian poet, painter and novelist

Love is the only force capable of turning an enemy into a friend.

MARTIN LUTHER KING, JR.
American clergyman, civil rights leader and Nobel Peace Prize winner

In our concern for others, we worry less about ourselves. When we worry less about ourselves an experience of our own suffering is less intense. What does this tell us? Firstly, because our every action has a universal dimension, a potential impact on others' happiness, ethics are necessary as a means to ensure that we do not harm others. Secondly, it tells us that genuine happiness consists in those spiritual qualities of love, compassion, patience, tolerance and forgiveness and so on. For it is these which provide both for our happiness and others' happiness.

THE DALAI LAMA
Tibetan Buddhist spiritual and temporal leader and winner of the Nobel Peace Prize

At some ideas you stand perplexed, especially at the sight of human sins, uncertain whether to combat it by force or by human love. Always decide, "I will combat it with human love." If you make up your mind about that once and for all, you can conquer the whole world. Loving humility is a terrible force; it is the strongest of all things and there is nothing like it.

FYODOR DOSTOYEVSKY
Russian novelist

I have never met a person whose greatest need was anything other than real, unconditional love. You can find it in a simple act of kindness toward someone who needs help. There is no mistaking love. You feel it in your heart. It is the common fiber of life, the flame of that heats our soul, energizes our spirit and supplies passion to our lives. It is our connection to God and to each other.

ELISABETH KüBLER-ROSS
Swiss-born psychiatrist, thanatologist and author

All works of love are works of peace.

MOTHER TERESA

Albanian Christian missionary in India and winner of the Nobel Peace Prize

Salaam
In the name of Allah, the beneficent, the merciful.
Praise be to the Lord of the Universe who has created us
and made us into tribes and nations
That we may know each other, not that
we may despise each other.
If the enemy incline towards peace, do
thou also incline towards peace, and
trust God, for the Lord is the one that
heareth and knoweth all things.
And the servants of God,
Most gracious are those who walk on
the Earth in humility, and when we
address them, we say "PEACE"

PEACE PRAYER FROM THE ISLAMIC TRADITION

Goodness is stronger than evil; Love is stronger than hate;
Light is stronger than darkness;
Victory is ours through he who loves us.

ARCHBISHOP DESMOND TUTU

South African clergyman, civil rights activist and winner of the Nobel Peace Prize

I am a man of peace. I believe in peace. But I do not want peace at
any price. I do not want the peace that you find in stone; I do not
want the peace that you find in the grave; but I do want the peace
which you find embedded in the human breast, which is exposed to
the arrows of the world, but which is protected from all harm by the
power of Almighty God.

MAHATMA GANDHI

(Mohandas K. Gandhi) Indian leader and peace activist

Hatred never ceases by hatred but by love alone is healed.
This is an ancient and eternal law.

THE BUDDHA

We who work for peace must not falter. We must continue to pray for peace and to act for peace in whatever way we can, we must continue to speak for peace and to live the way of peace; to inspire others, we must continue to think of peace and to know that peace is possible.

PEACE PILGRIM
American peace advocate, a.k.a. Mildred Norman Ryder

*Better than a thousand hollow words
is one word that brings peace.*

THE BUDDHA

*We must be prepared to make heroic sacrifices for the cause of peace that we make ungrudgingly for the cause of war.
There is no task that is more important or closer to my heart.*

ALBERT EINSTEIN
American physicist and Nobel laureate

To work in the world lovingly means that we are defining
what we will be for, rather than reacting
to what we are against.

CHRISTINA BALDWIN
American author of spiritual literature

Peace is not something you wish for:
it's something you make, something you do, something you are,
something you give away.

ROBERT FULGHUM
American author and Unitarian clergyman

Peace is not the product of terror or fear. Peace is not the silence of
cemeteries. Peace is not the silent result of violent repression. Peace
is the generous, tranquil contribution of all to the good of all. Peace
is dynamism. Peace is generosity. It is right and it is duty.

OSCAR ROMERO
Martyred Archbishop of El Salvador

Peace, like every other rare and precious thing,
doesn't come to you. You have to go and get it.

FAITH FORSYTE

English poet, a.k.a. Patience Strong

Those for whom peace is no more than a dream
are asleep to the future.

JACK DUVALL

American producer and nonviolent conflict author

Unless the cause of peace based on law gathers behind it the force
and zeal of a religion, it hardly can hope to succeed.

ALBERT EINSTEIN

American physicist and Nobel laureate

The only thing necessary for the triumph of evil
is for good men to do nothing.

EDMUND BURKE
British statesman and political thinker

Those who love peace must learn to organize as effectively
as those who love war.

MARTIN LUTHER KING, JR.
American clergyman, civil rights leader and Nobel Peace Prize winner

One little person, giving all of her time to peace, makes news.
Many people, giving some of their time, can make history.

PEACE PILGRIM
American peace advocate, a.k.a. Mildred Norman Ryder

Every day we do things, we are things, that have to do with peace. If we are aware of our lifestyle, our way of consuming, our way of looking at things, we will know how to make peace right in the moment we are alive.

THICH NHAT HANH
Vietnamese Buddhist monk and peace activist

We cannot have world peace without peace in our own lives. We cannot attack our planet by the way we live, and then go off to a peace rally and hope to set right all the imbalance we have caused. Peace is first a private matter. It cannot grow except from there.

GRANNY D
Doris "Granny D" Haddock, activist from New Hampshire

Talk peaceful to be peaceful.

NORMAN VINCENT PEALE
American religious leader

Our principle is, and our practices have always been, to seek peace, and ensue it, and to follow after righteousness and the knowledge of God, seeking the good and welfare, and doing that which tends to the peace of all...

QUAKER DECLARATION TO CHARLES II

Never doubt that a small group of thoughtful, committed citizens can change the world; indeed, it is the only thing that ever has.

MARGARET MEAD
American anthropologist

Your motives, if you are to find inner peace, must be an outgoing motive—it must be service. It must be giving, not getting.

PEACE PILGRIM
American peace advocate, a.k.a. Mildred Norman Ryder

From what we get, we can make a living;
what we give, however, makes a life.

ARTHUR ASHE
African-American tennis star and humanitarian

Peace is more the product of our day-to-day living than of a
spectacular program intermittently executed.

DWIGHT DAVID EISENHOWER
34th president of the United States

Peace is not the product of a victory or a command. It has no
finishing line, no final deadline, no fixed definition of achievement.
Peace is a never-ending process, the work of many decisions.

DR. OSCAR ARIAS
Former president of Costa Rica and winner of the Nobel Peace Prize

The journey of a thousand leagues begins with a single step. So we must never neglect any work of peace within our reach, however small.

ADLAI E. STEVENSON
American politician and vice president

There is no time left for anything but to make peace work a dimension of our every waking activity.

ELISE BOULDING
uaker peace activist, lecturer and networker

One day we must come to see that peace is not merely a distant goal we seek, but that it is a means by which we arrive at that goal. We must pursue peaceful ends through peaceful means.

MARTIN LUTHER KING, JR.
American clergyman, civil rights leader and Nobel Prize winner

Music has a role to play in spreading the word of peace.

BILLY BRAGG
English singer-songwriter and political activist

When peace is our priority, world peace will become our reality.

JOHN WORLDPEACE
American artist and peace advocate

There is a certain kind of peace that is not merely the absence of war. It is larger than that. The peace I am thinking of is not at the mercy of history's rule, nor is it a passive surrender to the status quo. The peace I am thinking of is the dance of an open mind when it engages another equally open one—an activity that occurs most naturally, most often in the reading/writing world we live in. Accessible as it is, this particular kind of peace warrants vigilance.

TONI MORRISON
American writer, teacher and editor

The dove of peace has become the ostrich of complacency.

JEANE KIRKPATRICK

American political scientist and first woman ambassador to the United Nations

All of us can work for peace. We can work right where we are, right within ourselves, because the more peace we have within our own lives, the more we can reflect into the outer situation.

PEACE PILGRIM

American peace advocate, a.k.a. Mildred Norman Ryder

If we are to teach real peace in this world, and if we are to carry on a real war against war, we shall have to begin with the children.

MAHATMA GANDHI

(Mohandas K. Gandhi) Indian leader and peace activist

What kind of peace do I mean? What kind of peace do we seek? Not a Pax Americana enforced on the world by American weapons of war. Not the peace of the grave or the security of the slave. I am talking about genuine peace, the kind of peace that makes life on earth worth living, the kind that enables men and nations to grow and to hope and to build a better life for their children—not merely peace for Americans but peace for all men and women—not merely peace in our time but peace for all time.

JOHN F. KENNEDY
35th president of the United States

There is no trust more sacred than the one the world holds with children. There is no duty more important than ensuring that their rights are respected, that their welfare is protected, that their lives are free from fear and want and that they grow up in peace.

KOFI A. ANNAN
Secretary-General of the United Nations, from Ghana

Treat the earth well,
It was not given to you by your parents,
It was loaned to you by your children—

PROVERB FROM AMERICAN INDIAN TRADITION

Peace is based on a respect for life, the spirit of reverence for life. Not only do we have to respect the lives of human beings, but we have to respect the lives of animals, vegetables and minerals. Rocks can be alive. A rock can be destroyed. The Earth also. The way we farm, the way we deal with our garbage, all these things are related to each other.

THICH NHAT HANH
Vietnamese Buddhist monk and peace activist

In this life we cannot all do great things;
we can only do small things with great love.

MOTHER TERESA
Albanian Christian missionary in India and winner of the Nobel Peace Prize

Wage peace with your breath.
Breathe in firemen and rubble, breathe out whole buildings
and flocks of red wing blackbirds.
Breathe in terrorists
and breathe out sleeping children and freshly mown fields.
Breathe in confusion and breathe out maple trees.
Breathe in the fallen and breathe out lifelong friendships intact.
Wage peace with your listening:
hearing sirens, pray loud.
Remember your tools: flower seeds, clothes pins, clean rivers.
Make soup. Play music, learn the word for thank you in three
languages. Learn to knit, and make a hat.
Think of chaos as dancing raspberries, imagine grief as the
outbreath of beauty or the gesture of fish. Swim for the other side.
Wage peace. Never has the world seemed so fresh and precious—
Have a cup of tea and rejoice.
Act as if armistice has already arrived.
Don't wait another minute.

JUDYTH HILL
American poet

The Art of Peace begins with you. Work on yourself and your appointed task in the Art of Peace. Everyone has a spirit that can be refined, a body that can be trained in some manner, a suitable path to follow. You are here for no other purpose than to realize your inner divinity and manifest your innate enlightenment. Foster peace in your own life and then apply the Art to all that you encounter.

MORIHEI UESHIBA
Japanese martial arts expert and founder of Aikido

Blessed are the peacemakers.

JESUS CHRIST
Holy Bible

PEACE & JUSTICE

If one member suffers, all suffer together.

LETTER OF APOSTLE PAUL
Holy Bible

Recognition of the inherent dignity and of the equal and inalienable rights of all members of the human family is the foundation of freedom, justice and peace in the world.

PREAMBLE, UNIVERSAL DECLARATION OF HUMAN RIGHTS

May I become at all times, both now and forever
A protector of those without protection
A guide for those who have lost their way
A ship for those with oceans to cross
A bridge for those with rivers to cross
A sanctuary for those in danger
A lamp for those without light
A place of refuge for those who lack shelter
And a servant to all in need.
For as long as space endures,
And for as long as living beings remain,
Until then may I, too, abide
To dispel the misery of the world.

SHANTIDEVA
Indian master

Oh Great Spirit of our Ancestors
I raise my pipe to you.
To your messengers the four winds, and
to Mother Earth who provides
for your children.
Give us the wisdom to teach our children
to love, to respect, and to be kind
to each other so that they may grow
with peace of mind
Let us learn to share all good things that
you provide for us on this Earth.

PEACE PRAYER FROM AMERICAN INDIAN TRADITION

It isn't enough to talk about peace. One must believe in it. And it isn't enough to believe in it. One must work at it. Justice cannot be for one side alone, but must be for both.

ELEANOR ROOSEVELT
Former first lady and wife of President Franklin D. Roosevelt

When we are really honest with ourselves we must admit that our lives are all that really belong to us. So, it is how we use our lives that determines what kind of men we are. It is my deepest belief that only by giving our lives do we find life. I am convinced that the truest act of courage, the strongest act of manliness is to sacrifice ourselves for others in a totally non-violent struggle for justice. To be a man is to suffer for others. God help us to be men!

CÉSAR CHÁVEZ
American labor leader and founder of the United Farm Workers Organizing Committee

No peace without justice, no justice without forgiveness. To pray for peace is to pray for justice, for a right-ordering of relations within and among nations and peoples. It is to pray for freedom, especially for the religious freedom that is a basic human and civil right of every individual. To pray for peace is to seek God's forgiveness, and to implore the courage to forgive those who have trespassed against us.

POPE JOHN PAUL II

Equal and exact justice to all men, of whatever state or persuasion, religious or political; peace, commerce, and honest friendship with all nations, — entangling alliances with none; the support of the State governments in all their rights, as the most competent administrations for our domestic concerns, and the surest bulwarks against anti-republican tendencies; the preservation of the general government in its whole constitutional vigour, as the sheet anchor of our peace at home and safety abroad;... freedom of religion; freedom of the press; freedom of person under the protection of the habeas corpus; and trial by juries impartially selected, — these principles form the bright constellation which has gone before us, and guided our steps through an age of revolution and reformation.

THOMAS JEFFERSON
3rd president of the United States

Stability and peace in our land will not come from the barrel of a gun, because peace without justice is an impossibility.

ARCHBISHOP DESMOND TUTU
South African clergyman, civil rights activist and winner of the Nobel Peace Prize

Peace is not merely a vacuum left by the ending of wars.
It is the creation of two eternal principles, justice and freedom.

JAMES SHOTWELL
Canadian historian and internationalist

You can't separate peace from freedom because
no one can be at peace unless he has his freedom.

MALCOLM X
African-American nationalist and Muslim leader

We may never be strong enough to be entirely nonviolent in thought
word and deed. But we must keep nonviolence as our goal and make
strong progress towards it. The attainment of freedom, whether for
a person, a nation or a world, must be in exact proportion to the
attainment of nonviolence for each.

MAHATMA GANDHI
(Mohandas K. Gandhi) Indian leader and peace activist

*True peace is not merely the absence of tension but
is the presence of justice and brotherhood.*

MARTIN LUTHER KING, JR.

American clergyman, civil rights leader and Nobel Peace Prize winner

Peace cannot be built on exclusivism, absolutism and intolerance.

MAHATMA GANDHI

(Mohandas K. Gandhi) Indian leader and peace activist

*A right is not what someone gives you;
it's what no one can take from you.*

RAMSEY CLARK

American political activist and former Attorney General

There must be no double-standard approach.
If there is a peace, it should be a peace for all.

SERGEI STEPASHIN
Former prime minister of Russia

America is not like a blanket—one piece of unbroken cloth, the
same color, the same texture, the same size.
America is more like a quilt—
many patches, many pieces, many colors, many sizes,
all woven and held together by a common thread.

JESSE JACKSON
American civil rights leader

Charity means love towards the neighbor and compassion, for
anyone who loves his neighbor as himself also has as much
compassion for him in his suffering as he does for himself in his own.

EMANUEL SWEDENBORG
Swedish scientist and mystic

We have believed—and we do believe now—
that freedom is indivisible, that peace is indivisible,
that economic prosperity is indivisible.

MAHATMA GANDHI
(Mohandas K. Gandhi) Indian leader and peace activist

The peace we seek cannot be our personal possession. We need to
find an inner peace which makes it possible for us to become one
with those who suffer, and to do something to help our brothers and
sisters, which is to say ourselves…This peace is not a barricade
which separates you from the world. On the contrary, this kind of
peace brings you into the world and empowers you to undertake
whatever you want to do to try to help.

THICH NHAT HANH
Vietnamese Buddhist monk and peace activist

Peace is the work of justice indirectly, in so far as justice removes the obstacles to peace; but it is the work of charity (love) directly, since charity, according to its very notion, causes peace.

THOMAS AQUINAS
Italian Catholic philosopher

…When we pray for world peace, do we think of all those killed by hunger or maimed by disease? To obtain peace, it is not enough that global fighting ceases. True peace begins the moment that an acceptable quality of life is attained by the world's underprivileged…

DR. OSCAR ARIAS
Former president of Costa Rica and winner of the Nobel Peace Prize

Strictly speaking, one cannot legislate love, but what one can do is legislate fairness and justice…

MAYA ANGELOU
African-American poet

In this new century, we must start from the understanding that peace belongs not only to states or peoples, but to each and every member of those communities. The sovereignty of States must no longer be used as a shield for gross violations of human rights. Peace must be made real and tangible in the daily existence of every individual in need. Peace must be sought, above all, because it is the condition for every member of the human family to live a life of dignity and security.

KOFI A. ANNAN
Secretary-General of the United Nations, from Ghana

There is enough for all. The earth is a generous mother; she will provide in plentiful abundance food for all her children if they will but cultivate her soil in justice and in peace.

BOURKE COEKRAN
writer

For many of us, we are always wanting more—we would be happier if we had such and such. Maybe we should pause for a moment and hear what some people in the third world countries would like to make them happier. 1.Having enough to eat so when you go to sleep at night your stomach doesn't ache. 2. Having shoes on your feet and any kind of clothing to keep the cold out. 3. Having a roof over your head. 4. Having the hope that you'll be lucky enough to get some kind of an education. 5. Believing that the dream of freedom, brotherhood, and peace for all mankind will someday come true.

ABIGAIL VAN BUREN
American journalist and advice columnist

*Earth provides enough to satisfy every man's need,
but not every man's greed.*

MAHATMA GANDHI
(Mohandas K. Gandhi) Indian leader and peace activist

I have the audacity to believe that peoples everywhere can have three meals a day for their bodies, education and culture of their minds, and dignity, equality, and freedom for their spirits. I believe that what self-centered men have torn down, men other-centered can build up. I still believe that one day mankind will bow before the altars of God and be crowned triumphant over war and bloodshed, and nonviolent redemptive goodwill will proclaim the rule of the land.

MARTIN LUTHER KING, JR.

American clergyman, civil rights leader and Nobel Peace Prize winner

Worldwide practice of Conservation and the fair and continued access by all nations to the resources they need are the two indispensable foundations of continuous plenty and of permanent peace.

GIFFORD PINCHOT

American forester, conservationist and public official

Your life and my life flow into each other as wave flows into wave, and unless there is peace and joy and freedom for you, there can be no real peace or joy or freedom for me. To see reality—not as we expect it to be but as it is—is to see that unless we live for each other and in and through each other, we do not really live very satisfactorily; that there can really be life only where there really is, in just this sense, love.

FREDERICK BUECHNER
American author and theologian

Cooperation is the thorough conviction that nobody can get there unless everybody gets there.

VIRGINIA BURDEN
American self-help author and non-profit advocate

Our only hope today lies in our ability to recapture the revolutionary spirit and go out into a sometimes hostile world declaring eternal hostility to poverty, racism, and militarism. This call for a world-wide fellowship that lifts neighborly concern beyond one's tribe, race, class, and nation is in reality a call for an all-embracing and unconditional love for all men and women.

MARTIN LUTHER KING, JR.
American clergyman, civil rights leader and Nobel Peace Prize winner

All wars are civil wars, because all men are brothers.

FRANCOIS FENELON
French writer and liberal theologian

All men are brothers, like the seas throughout the world;
So why do winds and waves clash so fiercely everywhere?

EMPEROR HIROHITO
124th emperor of Japan

Peace comes from being able to contribute the best that we have, and all that we are, toward creating a world that supports everyone. But it is also securing the space for others to contribute the best that they have and all that they are.

HAFSAT ABIOLA
Nigerian activist for human rights

Freedom is indivisible, and when one man is enslaved, all are not free.

JOHN F. KENNEDY
35th president of the United States

I refuse to accept the view that mankind is so tragically bound to the starless midnight of racism and war that the bright daybreak of peace and brotherhood can never become a reality

MARTIN LUTHER KING, JR.
American clergyman, civil rights leader and Nobel Peace Prize winner

BARRIERS TO PEACE

The Art of Peace is not easy. It is a fight to the finish, the slaying of evil desires and all falsehood within. On occasion the Voice of Peace resounds like thunder, jolting human beings out of their stupor. The world will continue to change dramatically, but fighting and war can destroy us utterly. What we need now are techniques of harmony, not those of contention. The Art of Peace is required, not the Art of War.

MORIHEI UESHIBA
Japanese martial arts expert and founder of Aikido

We have learned to fly the air like birds and swim the sea like fish, but we have not learned the simple art of living together as brothers. Our abundance has brought us neither peace of mind nor serenity of spirit.

MARTIN LUTHER KING, JR.
American clergyman, civil rights leader and Nobel Peace Prize winner

Everybody today seems to be in such a terrible rush; anxious for greater developments and greater wishes and so on; so that children have very little time for their parents; parents have very little time for each other; and the home begins the disruption of the peace of the world.

MOTHER TERESA
Albanian Christian missionary in India and winner of the Nobel Peace Prize

Forgive do I creatures all,
and let all creatures forgive me.
Unto all have I amity, and onto none enmity.
Know that violence is the root cause of
all miseries in the world.
Violence, in fact, is the knot of bondage.
"Do not injure any living being."
This is the eternal, perennial, and unalterable
way of spiritual life.
A weapon, howsoever powerful it may be,
can always be superseded by a superior one;
but no weapon can, however,
be superior to non-violence and love.

PEACE PRAYER FROM THE JANIST TRADTION

Peace is the harvest of love as war is the fruit of hate.

JOAN WALSH
American writer

Only when peace lives in each of us, will it live outside of us. We must be like wombs for a new harmony. When it is small, peace is fragile. Like a baby, it needs nurturing attention. We must protect peace from violence and perversion if it is to grow.

DENG MING DAO
Taosit master and writer

*Peace is the happy natural state of man;
war is corruption and disgrace.*

JAMES THOMSON
Scottish poet

*Wars begin in the minds of men, and in those minds,
love and compassion would have built the defenses of peace.*

U. THANT
Burmese diplomat and third secretary general of the United Nations

We have thought of peace as a letting go and war as a girding up. We have thought of peace as the passive and war as the active way of living. The opposite is true. War is not the most strenuous life. It is a kind of rest-cure compared to the task of reconciling our differences.

M. P. FOLLETT
American sociologist

Peace hath higher tests of manhood than battle ever knew.

JOHN GREENLEAF WHITTIER
American poet and writer

Peace is not only better than war, but infinitely more arduous.

GEORGE BERNARD SHAW
Irish playwright and essayist

... People think non-violence is really weak and non-militant. These are misconceptions that people have because they don't understand what non-violence means. Non-violence takes more guts, if I can put it bluntly, than violence. Most violence acts are accomplished by getting the opponent off guard, and it doesn't take that much character, I think, if one wants to do it.

CÉSAR CHÁVEZ

American labor leader and founder of the United Farm Workers Organizing Committee

The peaceful are the strong.

OLIVER WENDELL HOLMES

American writer

The more we sweat in peace the less we bleed in war.

VIJAYA LAKSHMI PANDIT

Indian diplomat

Would you end war? Create great Peace.

JAMES OPPENHEIM
American poet and writer

The real test of power is not the capacity to make war
but the capacity to prevent it.

ANNE O'HARE MCCORMICK
British-born American journalist

The real and lasting victories are those of peace, and not of war.

RALPH WALDO EMERSON
American author, minister and activist

Peace between countries must rest on the solid
foundation of love between individuals.

MAHATMA GANDHI
(Mohandas K. Gandhi) Indian leader and peace activist

A peace that comes from fear and not from the heart
is the opposite of peace.

GERSONIDES
French rabbi and philosopher

Peace is a very complicated concept. When the lion
gobbles up the lamb and wipes his lips, then there's peace.
Well, I ain't for that peace at all.

ABBIE HOFFMAN
American writer and radical activist

You can bomb the world into pieces,
but you can't bomb it into peace.

MICHAEL FRANTI
African-American hip hop artist

One cannot subdue a man by holding back his hands.
Lasting peace comes not from force.

DAVID BORENSTEIN

American, founder of www.quoteland.com and community activist

We have war when at least one of the parties to a conflict
wants something more than it wants peace.

JEANE KIRKPATRICK

American political scientist and first woman ambassador to the United Nations

The Art of Peace does not rely on brute force to succeed.

MORIHEI UESHIBA

Japanese martial arts expert and founder of Aikido

You are not going to get peace with millions of armed men. The chariot of peace cannot advance over a road littered with cannon.

DAVID LLOYD GEORGE
Former British Liberal statesman and prime minister

The God of Peace is never glorified by human violence.

THOMAS MERTON
Catholic monk and spiritual writer

An eye for an eye makes the whole world blind.

MAHATMA GANDHI
(Mohandas K. Gandhi) Indian leader and peace activist

You can't shake hands with a clenched fist.

INDIRA GANDHI
Indian stateswoman and prime minister

The more bombers, the less room for doves of peace.

NIKITA KHRUSHCHEV
Premier of the Soviet Union, 1958-1964

To suggest that war can prevent war is a base play on words and a despicable form of warmongering. The objective of any who sincerely believe in peace clearly must be to exhaust every honorable recourse in the effort to save the peace. The world has had ample evidence that war begets only conditions that beget further war.

RALPH BUNCHE
American civil rights activist, peace negotiator and winner of the Nobel Peace Prize

There never was a good war or a bad peace.

BENJAMIN FRANKLIN
American statesman, printer, writer and scientist

Fair peace is becoming to men, fierce anger belongs to beasts.

OVID
Roman poet

*One is left with the horrible feeling now that war settles nothing;
that to win a war is as disastrous as to lose one!*

AGATHA CHRISTIE
British mystery writer

*The insight that peace is the end of war, and that therefore a war is
the preparation for peace, is at least as old as Aristotle, and the
pretense that the aim of an armament race is to guard the peace is
even older, namely as old as the discovery of propaganda lies.*

HANNAH HRENDT
German-American philosopher

And so, to the end of history, murder shall breed murder,
always in the name of right and honor and peace,
until the gods are tired of blood
and create a race that can understand.

GEORGE BERNARD SHAW
Irish playwright and essayist

If you are required to kill someone today, on the promise of a political
leader that someone else shall live in peace tomorrow, believe me, you
are not only a double murderer, you are a suicide, too.

KATHERINE ANNE PORTER
American writer

The past is prophetic in that it asserts loudly that wars
are poor chisels for carving out peaceful tomorrows.

MARTIN LUTHER KING, JR.
American clergyman, civil rights leader and Nobel Peace Prize winner

Every gun that is made, every warship launched, every rocket fired signifies in the final sense, a theft from those who hunger and are not fed, those who are cold and are not clothed. This world in arms is not spending money alone. It is spending the sweat of its laborers, the genius of its scientists, the hopes of its children. This is not a way of life at all in any true sense. Under the clouds of war, it is humanity hanging on a cross of iron.

DWIGHT DAVID EISENHOWER
34th president of the United States

Give me the money that has been spent in war and I will clothe every man, woman, and child in an attire of which kings and queens will be proud. I will build a schoolhouse in every valley over the whole earth. I will crown every hillside with a place of worship consecrated to peace.

CHARLES SUMNER
U.S. senator from Massachusetts, 1851-1874

There's no honorable way to kill, no gentle way to destroy.
There is nothing good in war. Except its ending.

ABRAHAM LINCOLN
16th president of the United States

Perhaps this war will pass like the others which divided us, leaving
us dead, killing us along with the killers but the shame of this time
puts its burning fingers to our faces. Who will erase the ruthlessness
hidden in innocent blood? Poetry is an act of peace. Peace goes into
the making of a poet as flour goes into the making of bread.

PABLO NERUDA
Chilean poet

During times of war, hatred becomes quite respectable, even
though it has to masquerade often under the guise of patriotism.

HOWARD THURMAN
African-American spiritual advisor to Martin Luther King, Jr.

Patriots always talk of dying for their country
and never of killing for their country.

BERTRAND RUSSELL

Welsh philosopher, mathematician, prolific writer and public figure

I am not only a pacifist but a militant pacifist. I am willing to fight
for peace. Nothing will end war unless the people themselves refuse
to go to war.

ALBERT EINSTEIN

American physicist and Nobel laureate

The calamity of war, wherever, whenever and upon whomever
it descends, is a tragedy for the whole of humanity.

RAISA M. GORBACHEV

Wife of former Russian President Mikhail Gorbachev

When a new post-war generation has grown to puberty and to youth and to manhood and womanhood, it should read, and it should be realistically told, of the futility, the idiocy, the utter depravity of war. For that matter, this instruction could begin at the age of six with the taking of those toy guns out of those toy holsters and throwing them in the ash-cans where they belong.

EDNA FERBER
American writer

[In war], if we align ourselves with one side or the other, we will lose our chance to work for peace.

THICH NHAT HANH
Vietnamese Buddhist monk and peace activist

Peace depends ultimately not on political arrangements but on the conscience of mankind.

HENRY A. KISSINGER
56th secretary of state and winner of the Nobel Peace Prize

We have entered the Third Millennium through the gate of fire. If today, after September 11, we see better and we see farther, we will realize that humanity is indivisible.

KOFI A. ANNAN
Secretary-General of the United Nations, from Ghana

If it were all so simple! If only there were evil people somewhere insidiously committing evil deeds, and if it were necessary only to separate them from the rest of us and destroy them. But the line dividing good & evil cuts through the heart of every human being. And who is willing to destroy a piece of his own heart?

ALEKSANDR SOLZHENITSYN
Russian writer, political ideologist and winner of the Nobel Prize for Literature

We have failed to grasp the fact that mankind is becoming a single unit, and that for a unit to fight against itself is suicide.

HAVELOCK ELLIS
British physician, psychologist and writer

Neither should it ever happen that once more the avenues to peaceful change are blocked by usurpers who seek to take power away from the people, in pursuit of their own, ignoble purposes.

NELSON MANDELA
Civil rights activist, former president of South Africa and winner of the Nobel Peace Prize

We should not allow the peaceful nature of religion, true religion, to be negated by those who use religion to incite hatred, and as a means of pursuing violence.

ALHAJI DR. AHMAD TEJAN KABBAH
Former president of Sierra Leone

No war, not even to punish an aggressor, is a good thing. Today people must learn to take into account each others' interests, if only for the sake of their own survival. I do not believe that…the point where politics and simple human morality intersect is only idealism.

RAISA M. GORBACHEV
Wife of former Russian President Mikhail Gorbachev

War may sometimes be a necessary evil. But no matter how necessary, it is always an evil, never a good. We will not learn how to live together in peace by killing each other's children. The bond of our common humanity is stronger than the divisiveness of our fears and prejudices. God gives us the capacity for choice. We can choose to alleviate suffering. We can choose to work together for peace. We can make these changes — and we must.

JAMES EARL CARTER

39th president of the United States and winner of the Nobel Peace Prize

Our human situation no longer permits us to make armed dichotomies between those who are good and those who are evil, those who are right and those who are wrong. The first blow dealt to the enemy's children will sign the death warrant of our own.

MARGARET MEAD

American anthropologist

No one is so foolish as to prefer to peace, war, in which, instead of sons burying their fathers, fathers bury their sons.

CROESUS
Last king of Lydia

Over the bleached bones and jumbled residues of numerous civilizations are written the pathetic words, "Too late." There is an invisible book of life that faithfully records our vigilance or our neglect. "The moving finger writes, and having writ moves on..." We still have a choice today: nonviolent coexistence or violent co-annihilation. This may well be mankind's last chance to choose between chaos and community.

MARTIN LUTHER KING, JR.
American clergyman, civil rights leader and Nobel Peace Prize winner

The alternative to peace is not war. It is annihilation.

RAYMOND SWING
American journalist

Unconditional war can no longer lead to unconditional victory. It can no longer serve to settle disputes. It can no longer be of concern to great powers alone. For a nuclear disaster, spread by winds and waters and fear, could well engulf the great and the small, the rich and the poor, the committed and the uncommitted alike. Mankind must put an end to war or war will put an end to mankind.

JOHN F. KENNEDY
35th president of the United States

Before the terrifying prospects now available to humanity, we see even more clearly that peace is the only goal worth struggling for. This is no longer a prayer but a demand to be made by all peoples to their governments—a demand to choose definitively between hell and reason.

ALBERT CAMUS
French philosopher, novelist and playwright

Peace is the one condition of survival in this nuclear age.

ADLAI E. STEVENSON
American politician and vice president

The release of atomic energy has not created a new problem. It has merely made more urgent the necessity of solving an existing one.

ALBERT EINSTEIN
American physicist and Nobel laureate

There will one day spring from the brain of science a machine or force so fearful in its potentialities, so absolutely terrifying, that even man, the fighter, who will dare torture and death in order to inflict torture and death, will be appalled, and so abandon war forever.

THOMAS ALVA EDISON
American inventor

The lethal possibilities of atomic warfare in the future are frightening. My own feeling was that in being the first to use it, we had adopted an ethical standard common to the barbarians of the Dark Ages. I was not taught to make war in that fashion, and wars cannot be won by destroying women and children. We were the first to have this weapon in our possession, and the first to use it. There is a practical certainty that potential enemies will have it in the future and that atomic bombs will some time be used against us.

WILLIAM D. LEAHY
American naval officer and chief of staff to President Franklin D. Roosevelt

If men can develop weapons that are so terrifying as to make the thought of global war almost a sentence for suicide, you would think that man's intelligence and his comprehension...would include also his ability to find a peaceful solution.

DWIGHT DAVID EISENHOWER
34th president of the United States

It did not take atomic weapons to make man want peace, a peace that would last. But the atomic bomb was the turn of the screw. It has made the prospect of future war unendurable.

J. ROBERT OPPENHEIMER
American physicist, nicknamed the "Father of the Atomic Bomb"

If we don't end war, war will end us.

H. G. WELLS
English writer

The choice is no longer between violence and nonviolence. It is either nonviolence or nonexisitence...

MARTIN LUTHER KING, JR.
American clergyman, civil rights leader and Nobel Peace Prize winner

I know not with what weapons World War III will be fought,
but World War IV will be fought with sticks and stones.

ALBERT EINSTEIN
American physicist and Nobel laureate

…No battle is ever won…they are not even fought.
The field only reveals to man his own folly and despair,
and Victory is an illusion of philosophers and fools.

WILLIAM FAULKNER
American author and winner of Nobel Prize for Literature

As long as there is one upright man, as long as there is one
compassionate woman, the contagion may spread and the scene is
not desolate. Hope is the thing that is left us in a bad time.

E. B. WHITE
American writer and editor

It's really a wonder that I haven't dropped all my ideals, because they seem so absurd. Yet I keep them, because in spite of everything I still believe that people are really good at heart. I simply can't build my hopes on a foundation of confusion, misery and death. And yet I think this cruelty will end, and that peace and tranquility will return again.

ANNE FRANK
German-Jewish diarist of *The Diary Of Anne Frank*

And they shall beat their swords into plowshares, and their spears into pruning hooks; nation shall not lift up sword against nation, neither shall they learn war any more.

PROPHET ISAIAH
Holy Bible

PEACEFUL SOLUTIONS

Peace is not merely a distant goal that we seek,
but a means by which we arrive at that goal.

MARTIN LUTHER KING, JR.
American clergyman, civil rights leader and Nobel Peace Prize winner

I am not here as a public official, but as a citizen of a troubled world
who finds hope in a growing consensus that the generally accepted
goals of society are peace, freedom, human rights, environmental
quality, the alleviation of suffering and the rule of law.

JAMES EARL CARTER
39th president of the United States and winner of the Nobel Peace Prize

We, the peoples of the United Nations, determined to save succeeding generations from the scourge of war, which twice in our lifetime has brought untold sorrow to mankind, and to reaffirm faith in fundamental human rights, in the dignity and worth of the human person, in the equal right of men and women and of nations large and small.... And for these ends to practice tolerance and live together in peace with one another as good neighbors... have resolved to combine our efforts to accomplish these aims.

CHARTER OF THE UNITED NATIONS
Preamble

Let us pray for all peoples and cultures of the world, for all those who seek God in different religious ways. May there always be dialogue among them, may intolerance and contempt be extinguished, and together may they seek ways of concord and fraternity.

POPE JOHN PAUL II

It is of the very nature of peace to permit different people to do different things towards its establishment, to stress different ways of making it real, to honor a variety of gifts in the service of a common objective.

EDWARD LEROY LONG, JR.
American ethicist and writer

...peace is the healing and the elevating influence of the world...

WOODROW WILSON
28th president of the United States

The Art of Peace I practice has room for each of the world's eight million gods, and I cooperate with them all. The God of Peace is very great and enjoins all that is divine and enlightened in every land.

MORIHEI UESHIBA
Japanese martial arts expert and founder of Aikido

The real differences around the world today are not between Jews and Arabs; Protestants and Catholics; Muslims, Croats, and Serbs. The real differences are between those who embrace peace and those who would destroy it; between those who look to the future and those who cling to the past; between those who open their arms and those who are determined to clench their fists.

WILLIAM J. CLINTON
42nd president of the United States

We who know the art of prayer can change the vibration and magnetic psyche of the Earth. We can transform the wave of destruction into an ocean of peace through our prayer and through our meditation.

YOGI BHAJAN
Global leader in both the Sikh and interfaith communities and a master of Kundalini Yoga

The highest peace is the peace between opposites.

KABBALAH, JEWISH TRADITION

...The fourth is freedom from fear, which, translated into world terms, means a world-wide reduction of armaments to such a point and in such a thorough fashion that no nation will be in a position to commit an act of physical aggression against any neighbor— anywhere in the world. That is no vision of a distant millennium. It is a definite basis for a kind of world attainable in our own time and generation. That kind of world is the very antithesis of the so-called "new order" of tyranny which the dictators seek to create with the crash of a bomb...

FRANKLIN D. ROOSEVELT
32nd president of the United States

*Peace cannot be achieved through violence,
it can only be attained through understanding.*

RALPH WALDO EMERSON
American author, minister and activist

Somehow, we must transform the dynamics of the world power struggle from the negative nuclear arms race, which no one can win, to a positive contest to harness humanity's creative genius for the purpose of making peace and prosperity a reality for all the nations of the world. In short, we must shift the arms race into a peace race. If we have a will—and determination—to mount such a peace offensive, we will unlock hitherto tightly sealed doors of hope and transform our imminent cosmic elegy into a psalm of creative fulfillment.

MARTIN LUTHER KING, JR.
American clergyman, civil rights leader and Nobel Peace Prize winner

I like to believe that people in the long run are going to do more to promote peace than our governments. Indeed, I think that people want peace so much that one of these days governments had better get out of the way and let them have it.

DWIGHT DAVID EISENHOWER
34th president of the United States

It is better to win the peace and to lose the war.

BOB MARLEY

Jamaican reggae singer, guitarist and composer

We can gain no lasting peace if we approach it with suspicion and mistrust or with fear. We can gain it only if we proceed with the understanding, the confidence, and the courage which flow from conviction.

FRANKLIN D. ROOSEVELT

32nd president of the United States

Central to Jewish spirituality is the idea of tikkun olam, *the act of "repairing the world." Tikkun, to heal, repair and transform the world — our responsibility is to do this daily, in every big and little thing we do.*

TIKKUN, JEWISH TRADITION

History can never be covered up.

ZHU RONGJI
9th premier of the People's Republic of China

Let us take the risks of peace upon our lives,
not impose the risks of war upon the world.

QUAKER PROVERB

The problems of this world are so gigantic that some are paralysed by their own uncertainty. Courage and wisdom are needed to reach out above this sense of helplessness. Desire for vengeance against deeds of hatred offers no solution. An eye for an eye makes the world blind. If we wish to choose the other path, we will have to search for ways to break the spiral of animosity. To fight evil one must also recognize one's own responsibility. The values for which we stand must be expressed in the way we think of, and how we deal with, our fellow humans.

BEATRIX, QUEEN OF THE NETHERLANDS
Queen of the Netherlands since 1980

Every kind of peaceful cooperation among men is primarily based on mutual trust and only secondarily on institutions such as courts of justice and police.

ALBERT EINSTEIN

American physicist and Nobel laureate

Establishing lasting peace is the work of education; all politics can do is keep us out of war.

MARIA MONTESSORI

Italian physician and educator

The purpose of life is not to be happy. It is to be useful, to be honorable, to be compassionate, to have it make some difference that you have lived, and lived well.

RALPH WALDO EMERSON

American author, minister and activist

The peace process we all aim for will not necessarily be a result of the mere signing of a treaty or agreement. It must become a matter of our everyday lives, so that peace settles and lasts and becomes supported by everybody. We therefore have to give peace all the required care and preserve it and promote it.

HASSAN II, KING OF MOROCCO
Moroccan king from 1961–1999

Living out a witness to peace has to do with everyday choices about the work we do, the relationships we build, what part we take in politics, what we buy, how we raise our children. It is a matter of fostering relationships and structures—from personal to international—which are strong and healthy enough to contain conflict when it arises and allow its creative resolution.

MARY LOU LEAVITT
American Quaker writer and peace advocate

I am convinced that if we are to get on the right side of the world revolution, we as a nation must undergo a radical revolution of values. We must rapidly begin the shift from a "thing-oriented" society to a "person-oriented" society. When machines and computers, profit motives and property rights, are considered more important than people, the giant triplets of racism, materialism, and militarism are incapable of being conquered.

MARTIN LUTHER KING, JR.

American clergyman, civil rights leader and Nobel Peace Prize winner

If you want to work for world peace,
go home and love your families.

MOTHER TERESA

Albanian Christian missionary in India and winner of the Nobel Peace Prize

Peace is much more precious than a piece of land.

ANWAR AL-SADAT

Former president of Egypt and recipient of Nobel Peace Prize

God, grant me the serenity
to accept the things I cannot change;
the courage to change the things I can
and the wisdom to know the difference.

The Serenity Prayer

REINHOLD NIEBUHR
American Protestant theologian

Peace is: to live, to love, to learn, and leave a legacy with balance and joy. Peace is: cooperation rather than competition; to become part of a synergistic, living whole. Peace is: the development of our human endowments that empower us with character and competence in the moment of choice. Peace is: learning to listen and live by conscience.

STEPHEN R. COVEY
U.S. educator and leadership consultant

Oh Allah!
I consult You as You are all Knowing,
and I seek ability from Your power
and I ask You for Your great favor,
for You have power, but I do not,
and You have knowledge, but I do not,
and You know all hidden matters.
Oh Allah!
If You know that this matter is good for me in my religion,
my livelihood and my life in the Hereafter,
then make it easy and bless it;
and if You know that this matter is evil for me in my religion,
my livelihood and my life in the Hereafter,
then keep it away from me and keep me away from it,
And choose what is good for me wherever it is,
And make me pleased with it.

MUHAMMAD
Muslim prophet and founder of Islam

Having the wisdom to face the truth will bring us closer to peace.

MELODY BEATTIE
American author of self-help books

How is one to live a moral and compassionate existence when one is fully aware of the blood, the horror inherent in life, when one finds darkness not only in one's culture but within oneself? If there is a stage at which an individual life becomes truly adult, it must be when one grasps the irony in its unfolding and accepts responsibility for a life lived in the midst of such paradox. One must live in the middle of contradiction, because if all contradiction were eliminated at once life would collapse. There are simply no answers to some of the great pressing questions. You continue to live them out, making your life a worthy expression of leaning into the light.

BARRY LOPEZ
American author

The hope of a secure and livable world
lies with disciplined nonconformists
who are dedicated to justice, peace and brotherhood.

MARTIN LUTHER KING, JR.
American clergyman, civil rights leader and Nobel Peace Prize winner

There must be amidst all the confusions of the hour a tried and
undisturbed remnant of persons who will not become purveyors of
coercion and violence, who are ready to stand alone, if it is necessary,
for the way of peace and love among men.

RUFUS JONES
American philosopher, historian and social reformer

To see the right and not to do it is cowardice.

CONFUCIUS
Ancient Chinese philosopher

Peace demands the most heroic labor and the most difficult sacrifice. It demands greater heroism than war. It demands greater fidelity to the truth and a much more perfect purity of conscience. The Christian fight for peace is not to be confused with defeatism.

THOMAS MERTON
Catholic monk and spiritual writer

Nonviolence is the greatest force at the disposal of mankind. It is mightier than the mightiest weapon of destruction devised by the ingenuity of man.

MAHATMA GANDHI
(Mohandas K. Gandhi) Indian leader and peace activist

There is no such thing as defeat in non-violence.

CÉSAR CHÁVEZ
American labor leader and founder of the United Farm Workers Organizing Committee

A fifth point concerning nonviolent resistance is that it avoids not only external physical violence but also internal violence of spirit. The nonviolent resister not only refuses to shoot his opponent but he also refuses to hate him.

MARTIN LUTHER KING, JR.
American clergyman, civil rights leader and Nobel Peace Prize winner

A good soldier is not violent.
A good fighter is not angry.
A good winner is not vengeful
A good employer is humble.
This is known as the Virtue of not striving.
This is known as ability to deal with people.
This since ancient times has been known
as the ultimate unity with heaven.

TAO TE CHING
Taoist scripture

*The greatest conquerer is he
who overcomes the enemy without a blow.*

SUN TZU

Chinese author of the oldest military treatise in the world, *The Art of War*

*Non-violence leads to the highest ethics, which is the goal
of all evolution. Until we stop harming all other living beings,
we are still savages.*

THOMAS ALVA EDISON

American inventor

*If you want to make peace with your enemy, you have to
work with your enemy. Then he becomes your partner.*

NELSON MANDELA

Civil rights activist, former president of South Africa and winner of the Nobel Peace Prize

If you want to make peace, you don't talk to your friends.
You talk to your enemies.

MOSHE DAYAN
Israeli general and statesman

To wrong those we hate is to add fuel to our hatred. Conversely, to
treat an enemy with magnanimity is to blunt our hatred for him.

ERIC HOFFER
American social philosopher and writer

The best way to destroy an enemy is to make him a friend.

ABRAHAM LINCOLN
16th president of the United States

Friendship is the only cure for hatred, the only guarantee of peace.

THE BUDDHA

When you call yourself an Indian or a Muslim or a Christian or a European, or anything else, you are being violent. Do you see why it is violent? Because you are separating yourself from the rest of mankind. When you separate yourself by belief, by nationality, by tradition, it breeds violence. So a man who is trying to understand violence does not belong to any country, to any religion, to any political party or partial system; he is concerned with the total understanding of mankind.

JIDDU KRISHNAMURTI
Indian theosophist

*Those who are merciful have mercy shown them by
the Compassionate One, if you show mercy
to those who are in the earth,
He Who is in heaven will show mercy to you.*

MUHAMMAD
Muslim prophet and founder of Islam

Lord, make me an instrument of Thy peace;
where there is hatred, let me sow love;
where there is injury, pardon;
where there is doubt, faith;
where there is despair, hope;
where there is darkness, light;
and where there is sadness, joy.
O Divine Master,
grant that I may not so much seek
to be consoled, as to console;
to be understood, as to understand;
to be loved, as to love;
for it is in giving that we receive;
it is in pardoning that we are pardoned,
and it is in dying that we are born to eternal life.

PEACE PRAYER OF ST. FRANCIS

Patron saint of animals and the environment and founder of the Franciscan Order

Time has come, the time is now
When love of God may unite us all
Love of life is the universal call
We must recognize we are from the same clay
Live through the same breath, same God we obey.
Where there is religious ego, let compassion prevail
Where there is diversity, let unity excel
Where there is bigotry, let there be dignity
Where there is oppression, set people free.
Oh, Divine Master,
Teach me to serve and not want to be served
Let the living truth live undisturbed
Still the drums of war, which cloud our perception
Let us hear your Word and follow your direction
Fill our hearts with love for your creation
Dissolve our fears, bring peace to every nation.
May our dawn bring us peace in the warlords' race
Eternal peace—St. Francis' grace.

YOGI BHAJAN

Global leader in both the Sikh and interfaith communities and a master of Kundalini Yoga

A human being is a part of the whole, called by us "Universe," a part limited in time and space. He experiences himself, his thoughts and feelings as something separated from the rest, a kind of optical delusion of his consciousness. This delusion is a kind of prison for us, restricting us to our personal desires and to affection for a few persons nearest to us. Our task must be to free ourselves from this prison by widening our circle of compassion to embrace all living creatures and the whole of nature in its beauty. Nobody is able to achieve this completely, but the striving for such achievement is in itself a part of the liberation and a foundation for inner security.

ALBERT EINSTEIN
American physicist and Nobel laureate

Compassion is not religious business, it is human business, it is not luxury, it is essential for our own peace and mental stability, it is essential for human survival.

THE DALAI LAMA
Tibetan Buddhist spiritual and temporal leader and winner of the Nobel Peace Prize

The Holy Prophet Mohammed came into this world and taught us:
"That man is a Muslim who never hurts anyone by word or deed,
but who works for the benefit and happiness of God's creatures.
Belief in God is to love one's fellow men."

ABDUL GHAFFAR KHAN
Afghan/Pathan leader, a.k.a "The Frontier Gandhi"

Lead me from death to life, from falsehood to truth;
Lead me from despair to hope, from fear to trust;
Lead me from hate to love, from war to peace;
Let peace fill our heart, our world, our universe

SATISH KUMAR
Indian editor and peace advocate

The basis of world peace is the teaching which runs through almost all the great religions of the world. "Love thy neighbor as thyself."

ELEANOR ROOSEVELT
Former first lady and wife of President Franklin D. Roosevelt

To love another person is to see the face of God.

VICTOR HUGO
French writer

INDEX

Clement of Rome, Saint (First Century AD) Pope, first ecclesiastical writer to be called Apostolic Father, 22

Clinton, William J. (1946–) 42nd president of the United States, 110

Coekran, Bourke (1854–1923) writer, 74

Cohen, Rabbi Kenneth L. (1952–) American writer and peace activist, 11

Confucius (551–479 BC) Ancient Chinese philosopher, 121

Covey, Stephen R. (1932–) U.S. educator and leadership consultant, 118

Crazy Horse (1849–1877) Oglala Sioux chief, 12

Croesus (ca. 560–546 BC) Last king of Lydia, 100

Dalai Lama, The (1935–) Tibetan Buddhist spiritual and temporal leader and winner of the Nobel Peace Prize, 20, 23, 26, 39, 43, 46, 129

Dayan, Moshe (1915–1981) Israeli general and statesman, 125

Deng Ming Dao, Taoist master and author, 83

Dostoyevsky, Fyodor (1821–1881) Russian novelist, 47

Significant & Sacred Texts & Traditions Quoted

ABOUT THE AUTHOR

TAMMY RUGGLES, after becoming legally blind with RP (retinitis pigmentosa), began writing when she was forced to retire from her social work job. In 2002 her local newspaper in rural Kentucky gave her a column of her own. Since then she has had close to eighty articles, short fiction stories and online children's books published. She has contributed to several online entertainment magazines, including *Entertainment Insiders* and *Rock-n-Reel*, and she was host of About.com's weekly "ClassicTV Trivia Game."

Ruggles, who has a bachelor's degree in social work and a master's in adult ed/counseling, sees that the ending of one career was the beginning of another. She says, "I always wanted to be a social worker, and I always wanted to be a professional writer. People are lucky to have one dream come true. I'm fortunate to have had two. "

Asked what inspired her to do this book, Ruggles relates, "The coming of my first grandchild. I thought to myself, and still do, 'What kind of a world will my son be living in years from now? And my grandchild?' I want a peaceful world. We all do. But will we ever have it? This book is for everyone—children, teenagers, adults—who has ever yearned for peace, regardless of religion or race or politics. " Tammy Ruggles lives in a small town in Kentucky.